the cranberries

in your head

Stuart Bailie

PHOTOGRAPHS

© ALL ACTION *Pages: 30, 40, 44, 46-47, 54-55, 57, 60, 74, 79*

© REDFERNS *Pages: 8, 36-39, 68-69*

© RETNA *Pages: Cover, Back Cover, 3-4, 6, 9-14, 16, 19, 20-29, 31-35, 41-42, 45, 48-50, 53, 56, 58, 61-64, 66-67, 70, 73, 75-78, 79-80*

© REX FEATURES *Pages: 30, 41*

THIS EDITION PUBLISHED IN 1995 BY
UFO MUSIC LTD, LONDON, ENGLAND.

PRINTED AND BOUND IN GREAT BRITAIN BY
BUTLER & TANNER LTD, FROME AND LONDON

the cranberries

in your head

Stuart Bailie

UFO Music Ltd.

introduction

It is strange how events have the habit of coming full circle. In the winter of 1990 through to April 1991 UFO Music were signing up Charlie Watts from The Rolling Stones to collaborate with us on a beautiful book/CD package entitled *"From One Charlie"* (a tribute to Charlie Parker) when yet another demo tape arrived at our A&R desk. Unlike many other record companies, we play everything we are sent as bands often go to a lot of trouble to record them. This particular tape of a band called The Cranberries stood out distinctly in the midst of the hundreds we had played to date. The four songs on the demo tape, especially Linger, left no doubt in our minds that they were by far the best songs and the most beautiful voice that we had heard that year.

An immediate phone call to Xeric Studios, led to a meeting that was arranged just before the launch of Charlie Watts *"From One Charlie"*. Daniel Coxon and I flew out to Cork to see what the faces looked like behind the music. We were extremely surprised to find a very young band all seriously shy, no doubt wondering what all the fuss was about. They played a twenty minute set especially for us right there in Xeric Studios. Quite frankly we were quite taken aback and literally gobsmacked.

We immediately sat down in the waiting room to talk terms for signing them up on the spot.

The band were quick to point out that we had not broken a new act in as yet, and the only act we were trying to break in at the time were Sundial (now on Beggars Banquet). I pointed out how well the Charlie Watts project was going, they acknowledged its success. It seemed like we were actually getting somewhere.

We talked about recording an LP and two singles to which several letters were exchanged and recording budgets were talked about..

Unfortunately Island Records came in at this point and offered a very substantial advance, which we tried to match, however, all said and done Island Records had more money.

Mark Hayward

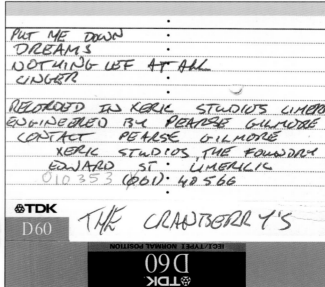

1
dreaming our dreams

Frankly, you never thought it would get so enormous. That this previously gawky tender-heart with the odd voice and weird accent would make such an amazing, glam-bam icon. That she'd reverse the pop fashion and prove that life can get more delicious and racy as you get older and more famous. That her band would sway millions of fans and out-perform all the other contenders, leaving thousands of them dead and 'berried in their trail.

So here's the poser. Where did it come from, all that class and gumption - her immaculate power to turn basic, sad words into life-changing creations? How did she capture the moment thus? To throw one of her famous lines back at her, Dolores O'Riordan: what's in your head?

That's just what an awful lot of people are thinking as the singer steps onto the tiny stage at Ronnie Scott's club in London's West End. Normally, this place is the preserve of cool jazz music. But on this special day - 14 September 1994 - we're getting a chance to see The Cranberries close up. We'll try and figure how they're becoming the biggest Irish act since U2. We'll hear songs from the band's critical second album. We'll witness another stage of Dolores'

painful, public development and catch that famous voice giving expression to her ever intense emotional life.

People in the audience gasp when they first see Dolores. Her hair's been cropped short and bleached to a shade of shiny platinum. That's not surprising by itself - she first appeared as a blonde at the Fleadh festival in London earlier in the Summer. Yet the visual shock of her hair has been heightened by styling it into a severe, masculine side parting. Then there's the small matter of her dressing up as a bloke...

She's wearing a black suit with braces, set off by a fat tie with geometric patterns. She's also put on a gent's pleated dress shirt that's so long in the arms that the cuffs have to be folded over twice. All this makes Dolores appear strong and sussed - her only feminine aspect is the row of gold rings, nine in all, which follow the curve of her right ear. Dolores looks like David Bowie in 1976, when he reinvented himself as The Thin White Duke, a decadent aristocrat. She also resembles the greatest gender-bender of this century, Marlene Deitrich

Noel, Mike and Feargal, they look remarkable too - they're decked out in suave three button jackets and trousers that were especially

commissioned from a Limerick menswear shop. Their hair is also cropped and it makes them look distinctively modish. This 1960s flashback will be heightened when they appear later wearing Harrington jackets and Fred Perry shirts. Noel will look like the double of Graham from Blur. Only more famous and successful.

At the Fleadh festival back in June - when almost 30,000 people crowded into a North London park to celebrate a full day's celebration of Irish music and culture, The Cranberries gave the first real indication of their desire to rework the band sound, to experiment and diversify. They shared the stage with string section, turning familiar songs into surprisingly grand statements. It was then that you realised that the band was never going to be just an *'indie'* act or an *'Irish'* group again - that their ambitions were far bigger than any of that. The only issue now was whether this new attitude - mixing guitar music with cello and catgut, draping your sound monitors with black satin and mixing baroque with your roll wasn't just going to fizzle out into pretentious nonsense.

As if to answer these misgivings, the Ronnie Scott's gig will take the band to the other musical extreme - to a simple, pared-down sound that will severely test the merits of the songs. Mike plays an acoustic bass, Noel favours a Spanish guitar, and Dolores likewise.

There's even a set of bongo drums put to one side, should Feargal chose to step away from his basic drum kit. The only real concession to the electronic age is a small Korg synthesiser which Dolores will play from time to time.

It's in this raw, intimate setting that you first hear *'Ode To My Family'*. And you've never heard such a song before in your life. Rock and roll is normally about burning up the past, severing the ties, leaving home and never looking back. Jim Morrison from The Doors expressed adolescent angst most directly when he sang, ***"father, I want to kill you"***. But not Dolores. This 23 year old has an entirely different take on the matter.

Her song deals with the pressures of success and the problems it causes in your hometown. It's about wanting to belong. Dolores wrote it after she'd been heckled repeatedly in Limerick. People would come up to her in bars and tell her how much they hated her. Begrudgers would shout *'bitch'* and *'rock star'* at her in the street. It got to the stage that Dolores would even dread meeting her parents and brothers and sister after a tour in case someone started talking about how much she'd changed. None of this happened in the old days, and Dolores never really wanted this new era. Like she sings in the song, *"It Wasn't My Design"*. It just happened, really.

So this song is her answer, a call for understanding. She still loves them all, and she's actually lonely and sad much of the time when people figure she's a stuck-up starlet. It's a brave admission, a rare kind of song that you would hardly ever get from a hip *'indie'* band. The band's British contemporaries would joke around the subject, douse it all with irony, keep you guessing. But The Cranberries don't shy away from these subjects. It's one of the reasons why they've attracted so many devoted fans - why American kids will throw their arms around Dolores and weep openly when they meet her, recognising a like-minded soul.

Dolores has the ability to cut through all of the distractions, to exocet your most hidden feelings. She even manages it at Ronnie Scott's, where half of those assembled are case hardened business folk - agents and journalists and radio people. She sings another new song called *"Empty"*, about being in the wake of a bitter relationship. She relates how she's lost her sense of indentity. All of her purpose has gone, her future plans are in bits. The words are simple, but Dolores keeps repeating the title, twisting the syllables, turning it upside down, trying to find meaning in the space around the words. By the finish of it, she's exhausted and the audience is wowing at the passion of it all.

We hear many of the songs from the new record - a lot of them exceptional, nothing to suggest that the band have lost anything in their tough rise to fame. If their first collection of songs was marked by insecurity and modesty, then these new creations are more determined, they have powerful themes and canny arrangements. One song in particular will scorch itself into everyone's imagination.

It's near the close we hear *"No Need To Argue"*. This is the song that Dolores takes most pride in - its simple, church-like tune reminds her of her childhood. The words are more upsetting though, as she sets out the predicament between herself and her partner. She's gone past the hurt and the upset, and now she knows they have to split up. Dolores remembers the good times; the two of them lying around together watching the TV, before all the arguments and the hatred. But all that's sadly, emphatically over now. When you look up at her face, there are literally tears in the singer's eyes.

Her husband of two months, Don Burton, stands discreetly to the left of the stage to escort Dolores off. When she exits, the audience is temporarily quiet, stunned by what they've all seen. Then everybody concurs. This is amazing stuff, they say. It's so pure and from the heart - the kind of music that will work its way into the soundtrack of your life, that you'll never forget. This album will do fantastically well, everybody agrees. It's inarguable, really.

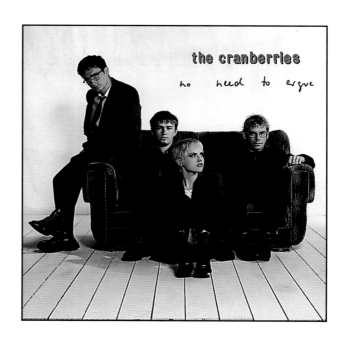

2 linger

On the cover of *'Linger'*, The Cranberries 1993 single, there's a photo of a little girl, dressed in her best Sunday pinafore and shoes, sitting on a stool by the church organ. It's an idealised version of Dolores' own childhood. This image helps to explain her attitude to music - why Dolores' voice is unique in the pop world, and why she has a different value system to most other performers.

You can hear her favourite music seep into the title track of the second album - the song deliberately echoes the church sounds that enthralled her from an early age. She loved the choir, especially when they performed the ancient Gregorian chants. She even learnt to sing and play keyboards and visited other churches to hear their chanting - that was her thing instead of teenybop bands. It's also an area of music that Dolores would like to pursue again in some far-off, solo project.

"The way that 'No Need To Argue' is just vocals and organ basslines," she tells you, *"it's really different, and I like that. That would be my messing around kind of music in the future. I was into the church and traditional Irish music, and the rest of the band weren't into any of that. I have all these influences, and fortunately that's what's made The Cranberries what they are.*

"I'd go to the pub and listen to country and western with my dad - 'Yellow Rose Of Texas' and all those kind of things, whereas the boys were into Everything But the Girl and all those modern bands. When I met them, I was saying, so, are there still bands apart from the big Top Of The Pops bands? And they'd say, yeah, it's called the indie scene. I didn't even know it existed.

"I've always had this longing to go back and do this other kind of stuff. And I will, you know."

There were six other kids in Dolores' family. A further two children died shortly after being born. As reported in Rolling Stone magazine, all this happened before Dolores' mother was 28. Mum then had to go to work as a caterer when her husband was injured in a motorcycle accident.

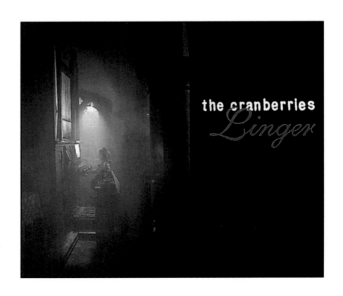

Life in the O'Riordan household in Ballybricken (a village eight miles outside Limerick) was also complicated when Dolores' big sister accidentally set the house on fire. The family was rescued by the good-will of their neighbours, who helped them move to a new place. Dolores had another lucky escape when she accidentally knocked a chainsaw down from the barn roof, leaving her with a gash in her head that required stitches.

Dolores skipped careers advice at school because she'd already decided she was going to sing for a living. She claims to have written her first song when she was 12. It was about an impossible crush she had for a much older man, and she titled in *'Calling'*. She described herself as a tomboy at this time, hanging out with a group of boys, wearing her hair short, getting into trouble at school for wearing ear-rings. Then, when adolescence kicked in hard, she found herself getting into difficult scrapes with some of the boys from this gang.

"I got into relationships with them and it was weird," she told NME in 1991. *"I wanted love straight away, but if I showed affection, they ran away. I had a horrible experience with every one of them. Guys would just break my heart."*

When you think of loser figures in pop (she even went through a period of fancying *"lunatics"*, and figured to her future embarrassment that Limerick lad Terry Wogan was *"quite good looking"*), then you normally picture the bedroom romantic, wallowing in misery, retreating to the world of the imagination and books. But the latter pastime certainly didn't figure in Dolores' world; even now she distrusts the written word, relying on her own instincts.

"I'm not bookish," she says. *"I prefer to have my own ideas. I'm not a big reader - I'd rather not develop my philosophies through someone else's writing. I'd rather understand it through life rather than have it formed by a book."*

She sang a bit with a few local bands, but they weren't ambitious at all, preferring to play safe versions of chart hits. When she was 18, Dolores left home and moved a flat in Limerick town, living cheaply, often going without proper food. She took up casual work to pay the bills, but was looking for a proper band to get busy with. Then she met up with The Cranberry Saw-Us.

Saucy name, saucy ex-singer. The departing frontperson was called Niall, and he was actually a distant acquaintance of Dolores. He was zany where Dolores was straight - giving the band their silly pun of a name, and writing ridiculous songs about family accidents and religious trauma. Apparently, his departure from the group wasn't such a bitter move, and he still gives his ex-colleagues the thumbs-up when he sees them back home.

Of the remaining members, Noel Hogan played guitar, and his brother Mike was the bassist. The drummer was Feargal Lawler, and Dolores was initially in awe of them because they seemed like city slickers, wise in the ways of the music business. They'd all got into rock and roll through an unconventional route - the breakdancing craze of the mid-'80s - but by 1990 they were hip to alternative rock - to bands like The Smiths and Everything But The Girl, and UK record labels like 4AD and Dedicated.

The boys were also keen to give up their day jobs. Feargal was a hairdresser. Mike had spent some time in a bakery and had taken a course in electronics. Noel was wasting his days on a youth employment scheme. Part of his training comprised of a section called the *'banana course'*. It was supposed to teach these young job hunters how to use a telephone properly, but since the scheme was lacking in basic equipment, some of the boys had to hold bananas to their ears instead of receivers. Early band rehearsals were loud and thrashy - Niall's barmy legacy took some time to overcome - and in the absence of any real songs, the three boys gave Dolores a tape of instrumental music. They hoped that she'd try to come up with a suitable idea - words, or a chorus or something. Instead, Dolores gave them *'Linger'*.

It was an amazing piece of work, and one that

set a precedent for simple but brutally honest confession songs. *'Linger'* was apparently written about a teenage boyfriend who'd left Dolores to join the army and serve in the Lebanon. The words of the song didn't make for great literature (the last time a pop band rhymed *'linger'* and *'finger'* was the Bay City Rollers' *'Bye Bye Baby'* in the early '70s), but it worked perfectly with a low-key band arrangement and Dolores' wistful tones.

That was her strength already. She could take the simplest phrase and bend the words around until she broke your heart. She'd repeat a key word again and again until it took on huge significance - more compelling than the

cleverest chorus. Meanwhile, her training in church and knowledge of folk music allowed her the chance to play with some vocal styles that were rarely used in rock music.

She would sing clearly and unhurriedly, letting her words echo around the walls like an old Gregorian chorister. And like the practitioners of Irish folk songs (in particular, those who sang in the old unaccompanied style or sean-nos way), she would use ornamentation in her singing; swooping around an important word, hitting a series of related notes or jumping up an octave in mid-syllable. The latter technique is known as melisma. Sinead O'

Connor, who was also exposed to folk music as a child, uses it too. Dolores is continually being compared to the older singer, but critics often miss the fact that they're both getting their ideas from the same source, not copying from each other.

The boys were delighted with the way the new ideas were evolving. They had been aiming for a "softer music" and now they'd found the ideal singer. One of their models at this stage was the debut album from American singer Edie Brickell. They liked the way her songs like 'Circle' and 'What I Am' were so free and uncluttered. This would be their style too.

They fell in with the people who ran Xeric recording studios in town, and put together a three track tape, titled *'Nothing Left At All'*. They put it on sale locally, shifting 300 copies. In keeping with the dreamy music, the inlay card pictured a dolphin breaking over the waves on a moonlit sea, while on the back, the legend read **'LOVE IS AN ILLUSION'**. Some tapes were also sent to record companies in London, prompting interest from the very start.

Listening back to the tape, you can hear that Dolores' voice is already well formed. The music is a little clumsy, and there are some strange experiments with background noise and guitar harmonics which add little to the songs themselves. *'Nothing Left At All'* is the classic Dolores storyline - she's in the throes of

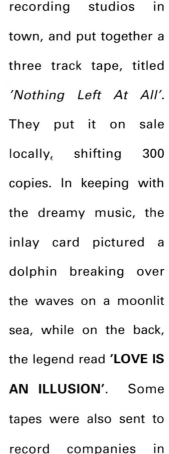

breaking up with a lover, knowing that whatever she does, it will cause her heartbreak. You can hear her rural Irish accent right away, a sign of artistic self-confidence that will really distinguish her later on.

'Pathetic Senses' is more up-beat with twee synth chords and male backing vocals. Dolores is trying to make a friend liven up and enjoy life; time is passing quickly, and they should have fun while they can. on 'Shine Down', the pace drops again. Noel strums lightly on an acoustic guitar. Dolores sings as the loser in love once again. A boy is running away from emotional commitments, and she can't understand why he should be so shallow, so thoughtless.

Record company interest quickened all the

way through 1990 as the band played their first nervous shows in Limerick and Dublin. By April '91, the attention had become fierce - one show was supposedly attended by more than 30 people from London - most of them keen to sign up a deal with the band.

The Cranberries' business affairs were being handled at the time by the people at Xeric Studios, who involved themselves in almost every stage of the band's development; recording, photographs, promotion, management. In the short-term, this attention to detail would work in the band's favour. But as the scale of the pressure became greater, the band's loyalties were confused, and they were pitched into anxious debates, legal action and the band's first sticky patch. Misery on an epic scale...

3 disappointment

Barely a year from when they'd first met, The Cranberries had signed a major deal to the American branch of Island records. It was the kind of offer most bands would never get a sniff of. Yet Dolores remembers the later half of 1991 as a period of much unhappiness and a virtual nervous breakdown.

"There were business difficulties," she tells you. *"It all got very twisted and I got depressed. You know when you're that age, you really need to learn, and you get a few kicks in the arse."*

She decided she was going to leave the band on one occasion. She became so thin-skinned that she'd burst into tears without warning. There was also a period of weeks when she became bed-ridden, she *"freaked"* completely. Talking to Melody Maker three years after the event, she described these times as *"my baby version of what happened to Kurt Cobain, and to Sinead O'Connor."*

The band's debut EP, *'Uncertain'* was disappointing as well. Two of the tracks, *'Nothing Left At All'* and *'Pathetic Senses'* had already appeared on their tape (the former was the same recording, the latter had some funky white noise added to the song). As for fresh

material, many insiders had already heard demo versions of *'Linger'* and *'Dreams'*, so they felt that *'Uncertain'* itself was a scrap of an idea in comparison.

Of all the songs, *'Them'* was the most interesting. It was written about a family feud, and the hushed, spooky tones certainly suggest impending aggravation. Dolores had left home in troubled circumstances the previous year - there are suggestions of a rough exchange between her punk boyfriend and some of her brothers.

There was conflict of a different sort when it came to presenting the band. The Cranberries were ill-prepared for their first real meetings with the press. Many Dublin-based journalists couldn't relate to the band's folksy element, and in turn, the group felt ill-at-ease in the capital. To the more intolerant Dubs, Limerick was only famous for unemployment and violence - nothing good ever came out of *'Stab City'*, especially music. Feargal later told Vox magazine about the culture clash between the unassuming Cranberries and the rock and roll wannabes of Dublin.

"There are bands - you see quite a lot of them in Dublin - who've made one album that hasn't

even gone anywhere, and they're walking around in cowboy boots and leather trousers with sunglasses on indoors, walking into fuckin' walls. I hate people like that, I really do."

The British press was no more helpful. The band members were often painted as cute country folk. There was a notorious feature that portrayed Dolores as this holy innocent - like Sister Maria in The Sound Of Music - communing with nature and bounding over the hill-tops with a song in her heart. Patronising nonsense.

"If you're working class and you're from Ireland," Dolores tells you, still pained at the memory of this treatment, **"they put you in a**

bracket, and the subtext of that is that Ireland equals a bog. They'll wave the charming, folkloric side and not realise that the Irish education system is better, that Irish people generally have more information than English people. It's quite insulting and it applies to the class system as well. If you're working class, then you're some kind of barrow boy. It's all a way of keeping you under control.

"It's all to do with where you come from and what your background is. And people that do that to me, they're not even worth commenting on. They're a waste of time. And it did get to me for a while. And then I got through to

somewhere in my head where I thought, these people are worthless."

The first journalists who tried to discover what was going on inside Dolores' head found some bits of startling information. Talking to NME in 1991, she revealed that she indulged in binge eating, scoffing up to 26 packets of crisps in a day. When queried about the affairs of her country, she defended the Church's influence in Ireland, saying, *"they're doing a grand job; some people, think they brainwash people, but if the public wanted rid of them, they'd be gone."*

Dolores came across in the papers as a combination of the maternal and the neurotic.

She fretted over the alcohol intake of the boys in the band, and discouraged people smoking joints backstage, saying the smell of it was like *"vomit"*. She talked about her surprise at walking the streets of London and seeing so many *"different races"*. It all seemed absurdly naive. And while Dolores matured quickly and broadened her perspective on life, she never spoke so openly again as the days when she was 18 and fresh to the interview experience.

"It seemed as though we were being ridiculed by some very small-minded Englishmen," a wiser Dolores told the NME in 1994. *"I was reading some stupid crap about me."*

As a result of these strange conversations and the incredulous responses of the journalists, there was a major falling out between the band and the press. The poor quality of 'Uncertain' didn't help the two sides to make up. Nor did the silly criticisms in some of the English papers, which downgraded the band for supposedly ripping off the Home Counties' "shoegazing" bands - a faddish indie cult whereby faceless long-hairs would twiddle with effects pedals and fashion a cloud of guitar noise around the wisp of a song.

Another band name, The Sundays, was frequently evoked. The Sundays were heavily influenced by The Smiths, and featured warbling female vocals. Dolores claims she'd never heard of them - though she later went to one of their shows to see what she'd

supposedly ripped off.

"I went to see The Sundays," she told Mojo magazine, *"and came out of the gig with a smile on my face from ear to ear. They weren't a bit like us."*

From this point on, The Cranberries sensed it might have to be America, or bust.

4
everybody else is doing it...

The following year, 1992, wouldn't be such a fun year either. By now, the band and management weren't relating so well. According to Dolores, there was a lot of suspicion and misunderstanding. Everybody seemed to be walking around with a different agenda, a contrary version of the events that were unfolding.

They tried to record three tracks for the album in the Limerick studio, but everyone was too tense, and the attempts to bring in dance rhythms and experimental noise were becoming a distraction. Finally, The Cranberries got rid of their old business team and shifted their dealings to Rough Trade Management in London.

"When we fired our manager," Dolores told Rolling Stone, *"I think it made us a lot stronger. I knew I would never again let anyone make me do something I didn't want to do."*

They moved the recording to Windmill Lane in Dublin, and began working with producer Stephen Street, who'd made his reputation with the later Smiths LPs and then Morrissey's solo career. He restored morale, gave a shine to their still-fragile sound, and readied them up for success in America with a few choice arrangements and harmonies.

Songs like *'Linger'* and *'Dreams'* had been in the repertoire for almost two years by the time they were properly recorded. Other songs like *'Pretty'*, with its refrain of *"you won't change me"*, and *'Still Can't...'* were drawn from more recent spates of anguish - thinly-disguised attacks on people who'd tried to put the band down. *'Pretty'* went even further in that it exposed the back-handed compliments women are subjected to - encouraged to stay in the background, not to get overly independent.

So while the album title, *'Everybody Else Is Doing It, So Why Can't We?'* suggests a band of shy, deferential souls, The Cranberries had actually proven themselves to be hard fighters to make it thus far. They were stronger than the back-biters and detractors who've written them off, more durable that the sharpies who wanted to make them work to their own schemes. You can read the title another way too - that it signalled the band's readiness to go public at last.

The Cranberries' new confidence was reflected in their body language, in the way they related to each other. One day they were bunched up together on a couch in the record company when someone noticed how comfortable they all looked - like a gang in which everybody knew their place. Or even like a bunch of old flatmates - like The Young Ones, chilling out for an evening in front of the telly. A photo session was immediately convened, and the band had their image all ready for the record sleeve.

Unfortunately, the public were not so amenable. *'Dreams'* wasn't a hit on release in November '92. In February the following year they put out *'Linger'* and it only reached number 74 in the charts. When the album was released the following month, it managed no better, barely selling 10,000 copies. Suede and the new glam were exciting the indie scene, and the fashion-free Cranberries were passed over in the rush.

Fortunately, the band had discovered a passion for touring, something which many of the new bands lacked. The Cranberries supported Belly across the UK in March, followed by a European tour with the Hothouse Flowers. Their first American tour was soon after, opening for The The, and as 1993 was coming to an end, they saw more of America supporting Suede before spending October in the company of Duran Duran.

This was the saving of the band. They were keen and positive - qualities which didn't count for so much in the UK scene, where bands are encouraged to have an attitude and to sneer at the idea of slogging it out in the heartlands of America. But The Cranberries enjoyed all this, and the admiration was mutual. ***"I love the open-mindedness of the Americans,"*** Dolores said afterwards. ***"They're not so judgmental"***

And it was the Americans who were first excited about *'Linger'* which became a favourite on MTV as it lit up the regional radio stations, many of whom the band had taken time to visit during their hectic months of criss-crossing the country. Ultimately, it was a top ten hit, confirming Dolores' faith in its durability. ***"Patsy Cline might have sang it,"*** she told Mojo. ***"Although 'Linger' is a 1993 pop song, there's a timelessness about it, and that's why people reacted differently, because it's not fashion."***

The charm tactics were so successful that when the band played Atlanta with Suede, the bill had to be reversed, allowing the Irish band to headline. Soon, they were selling upwards of 70,000 copies of the album every week. By the end of the year, they'd shifted over 1.3 million. It was another humbling demonstration for the music business. A decade earlier, U2 followed the exact same route into the arms of America, playing hard and long, cultivating allies, finding loyal friends in the mid West, leaving much hipper bands like the Teardrop Explodes and Echo And The Bunnymen to stay and home and badmouth their way into oblivion.

'Everybody Else Is Doing It...' finished 1993 as the best-selling debut of any British or Irish band in that year. They'd even out-performed U2 in the record book; not even Bono's group managed to sell over a million copies of their debut record in the USA.

5 i will be with you

Dolores found all this hugely liberating. She grew confident on stage, enjoying the fan feedback, encouraged to make expansive gestures, to flounce and flirt in front of thousands of strangers. She explained this radical turnaround to Melody Maker in 1994.

"I knew there was so much to performing that was false, and I didn't like being in a position where a lot of people were looking at me, Dolores. I felt vulnerable up there. But then - it reversed! It became me being in control of it, and it became a brilliant thing to be there with everyone looking and me being able to take it and use it."

London witnessed this rebirth and the astonishing scenes that went with it on 14 January '94, at the Astoria 2 Club on Charing Cross Road. Dolores walked onto the stage with an American flag draped around her, beaming and totally loving the rapture that was welling up through the venue. *"We have returned!"* she gushed.

She looked like a real star now; a scarlet skull-cap, a Saint Patrick's cross around her neck, shorn hair, shorts and a lacy dress. The uncomfortable adolescent had evolved into a sleek, confident adult. She was gloriously in command of her art, laughing when boys yelled out marriage proposals, telling everyone about the band's success *"over there"*, playing guitar more frequently and launching into some Irish dancing in the instrumental break for *'Liar'*.

The band was stock-piling a set of new tunes as well - all those sound-checks across America had given them the opportunity to keep writing and changing. Many new bands often have to rush their second album, putting out a make-do product because they're strapped for time and fresh experiences. The Cranberries had plenty of both stored up. At the Astoria, they previewed seven numbers, including *'Dreaming My Dreams'* - a beautiful ballad in waltz time in which Dolores' sang of the joys of a stable relationship. America had witnessed another happy outcome for the band; while touring with Duran Duran, Dolores had become friendly with the latter's tour manager *"a fine six footer"* from Canada, Don Burton.

A show at Dublin's Tivoli theatre exacted the same kind of excitement and critical revisionism, as The Cranberries' ascent was endorsed everywhere. Both *'Dreams'* and then *'Linger'* were reissued in Britain, and this time they were widely appreciated. The debut album was re-promoted and TV-advertised too, and sold handsomely, reaching the very top of the chart in the summer. Only four other acts have managed to peak at such a belated stage (such a record is known in the trade as a *"sleeper"*) in British pop history.

The downside of this was the fact that Dolores became a proper celebrity. Her love life, her holiday destinations, her opinions on controversial topics, whose shirts she wore - these were all sought-after stories in the press, especially in Ireland. So when she damaged her leg during an Spring skiing holiday in the Alps, the rumour-mongers came up with many lurid versions of what really happened. She never hurt herself at all, some argued. She's just getting uppity, and doesn't want to tour for a while, a few 'experts' declared. Another favourite interpretation was that The Cranberries were under so much pressure, and hated each other so much that the break-up of the band was now only a formality. Dolores' 'accident' was just a ruse to buy time and to get them off the imminent Crowded House tour...

All wrong. The singer was suffering from a *"torn anterior cruciate ligament"*. The injury required surgery, metal pins inserted into bone, a fibreglass ligament fitted and a course of physiotherapy which was needed after muscle had set wrongly and needed to be pulled apart

again. She was left with a huge Y-shaped scar around her thigh and knee. Hardly a PR stunt or a phony injury.

Dolores was bed-ridden for a month, but actually found the experience to be useful. A period of reflection, followed a holiday in Jamaica, where she practiced walking again on the beach, helped to bring calm back into her life.

"I don't think I would be as happy now as I am with the band if that hadn't happened," she told NME in September. *"You can be doing things and not thinking. So I had a chance to have a good think about everything that has happened to us, and I decided that I wasn't going to go mental."*

By June, The Cranberries were playing again, though Dolores sat on a chair for parts of their Fleadh festival set. She also made some televisional appearances with Jah Wobble's band - her vocals on the latter's single, *'The Sun Does Rise'* were fresh and optimistic like never before, and the record was a hit.

"I have a tendency to write about negative things," she tells you, smiling. *"And that's one of the reasons I liked this song, because it's different for me. I'm just more inspired when I'm negative."*

Dolores didn't think that her July marriage would interest the press, but she was mistaken. Masses of photographers and journalists turned

up at the Holy Cross Abbey in Tiperary for the ceremony, gawping at her see-through dress, her lace leggings, the gemstone in her belly button, the ridiculously romantic sight of Dolores riding off with Don in a horse-drawn buggy. The writers duly filed stories, reporting that *"she'd got married in her knickers."*

Dolores was annoyed at the stories, especially the accusations that she was insensitive and tasteless in her approach to a religious service. She thought her critics were *"bitchy"*, but she also revealed to Hot Press magazine that her own father was taken aback by her outfit.

"My dad was funny because he's a real countryman. And I put on the outfit and said, look dad, and he said, 'yes, that's lovely, but where's the dress?' I said, dad, I'm not wearing a dress. I don't want to be boring and predictable. I want to wear something different."

The singer's attitude towards organised religion had evolved a lot since her teenage days. When you quizzed her about this in 1994, she was less supportive of the church, reserving the right to have mixed feelings.

"You can wake up one morning and take that whole perspective - that Jesus Christ was born of a human being. As a Catholic and a Christian, that's what you're taught to believe. And then some days you get up and everyone's just a wanker. The next day, you feel that Jesus is in everybody, so be nice to everyone. It depends on your own frame of mind."

zombie

The single *'Zombie'* was released in September. They knew it would be popular - American audiences were mad for it when they heard it live in '93. Dolores was confident that she'd written ***"a really powerful song"***. And when the band previewed it in Britain in January '94 - with the singer addressing the Astoria audience, telling them how much she cared about this particular message - the response was positive there too.

The theme of the song was certainly controversial. While an old Cranberries song like 'Pretty' was vaguely political, *'Zombie'* was a direct attack on the warmongers in Ireland, in particular, the supporters of the IRA. Her attack was made specific in the line, ***"It's the same old theme since 1916"***. This was the date of the Easter Rising in Ireland, a bloody event that led to the creation of the Irish Republic and the withdrawal of British troops from those 26 counties. But Dolores didn't want to commemorate old battles, to condone the patriot game, to watch the mounting death toll north of the border and beyond.

The video made this even more explicit. In bleak, monochrome footage, The Cranberries' team filmed British squaddies patrolling the peace line in West Belfast, alert and nervous. We saw political murals on the Falls Road, commemorating the Republican hunger strikers and calling for an end to the British presence in the Northern Ireland. The video also included shots of Protestant graffiti and murals, suggesting that the problems were not one-sided.

Weirdly, the band scenes were shot in Los Angeles. Dolores was daubed in gold paint and stood by a memorial cross, delivering her urgent message - chiefly that innocent people are being killed in the streets. In the lyrics, she can't begin to understand the mind-set of people who cause the death of children, who leave behind broken-hearted, grieving mothers. She sings desperately of the men with their tanks and bombs and guns - echoing the sad old folk song, *'Johnny, I Hardly Knew You'*. Finally she turns on the warlords and tries to understand their motives. ***'What's in your head?"*** she demands repeatedly, angry and disbelieving.

Dolores had written the song while touring Britain in 1993 - shortly after the Warrington bombing in England, when the IRA targeted a shopping centre, killing and wounding innocent school children.

"A lot of people need to grow up," she told NME a week before the record's release, *"If these adults have a problem with these other adults, well, go and fight them. But don't stick a bomb somewhere where you'll hurt kids and ordinary women who never did anything to you. Some people might think they're getting their point across, but to me... it's pathetic, really."*

Some people felt that these sentiments were well-meant, but were so vague and liberal that they wouldn't help anybody - as relevant as The Police's *'Invisible Sun'* or Spandau Ballet's *'Through The Barricades'.* Others thought it was a pompous overview of a deeply complex problem. The Derry thrash band Schtum, who'd experienced the problems of Ulster every day, all their lives, weren't impressed. *"She's from Limerick, what the fuck would she know?"* they told Melody Maker. *"You're talking about the last 25 years of a much bigger and wider problem that has gone on for hundreds of years."*

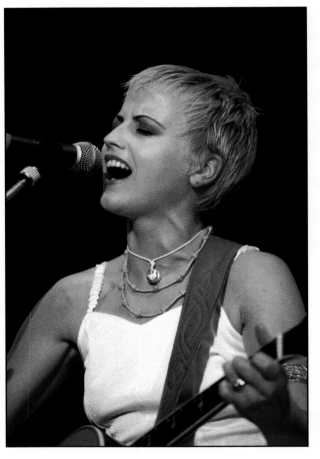

But Dolores was adamant that good-will and forgiveness were enough to solve the biggest problems. As she talked you though her personal peace formula, you were aware that the IRA had just then announced a ceasefire, and that the loyalist paramilitaries were also about to follow suit. *'Zombie'* might (very hopefully) go down in the books as the last record bemoaning 'The Troubles' before the onset of peace. That would be distinction enough.

"You should just let it go," she tells you. *"That's my thing in life; I get over experiences and write about them. Life's too short. The last four years of my life have gone so fast. I came over here when I was 18; now I'm 23. And it all feels like a year. People shouldn't fall out over countries and territory so much. It doesn't matter. You should look to your grave, and that's your country."*

7 no need to argue

The photo session for *'No Need To Argue'* involved a hilarious sofa safari around Dublin and the nearby coastline. The band started off by posing on this dingy piece of furniture (the same settee they'd used on the first LP cover) in the terraced streets of the capital. They stopped for more snaps outside a derelict boozer because it said *'Lounge'* on the sign, and funnily enough, there they were, getting comfy outside. They pulled up by the old gasworks because it looked cool and surreal. And as the day's work grew more absurd, The Cranberries steered through the rain to Dalkey Island on the south end of Dublin Bay, taking the increasingly soggy sofa with them in a little boat. At the finish of it all, they even managed to get a stunning picture of themselves cosying up, half-way out to sea, beneath a glorious big rainbow.

For the actual cover shot, the band sat around the sofa in a studio, consciously re-enacting the shot on *'Everybody Else Is Doing It...'*. In was an inspired piece of symbolism. On the first sleeve, the band looked gloomy, unkempt and camera shy. A year and a half later and you can see how their experiences have changed them - how they've developed from couch potatoes into confident, flourishing adults.

The songwriting had also come on. It wasn't so introverted now, Dolores was finding lots of new subjects to cover. For example, she wrote about the poet WB Yeats and his doomed love affair with the revolutionary Maud Gonne (Sinead O'Connor was also obsessed with this story, using it as the basis for her debut single, *'Troy'*). Dolores had of course, made her statement about paramilitaries in Ireland as well. And with *'The Icicle Melts'* she was trying to articulate the horror surrounding the death of two year old Jamie Bulger - abducted from a Liverpool shopping mall and killed by two older children. The nature of evil was a recurrent theme on the record, and in later interviews, Dolores would suggest that the death sentence should be reinstated for those convicted of murder.

The Cranberries expressed their homesickness and tourbus blues on songs like *'So Cold In Ireland'* and *'Ode To My Family'*. The break-up of a relationship at the end of '93 provided Dolores with much emotional material, like *'Disappointment'*. On the lyric sheet to this song, Dolores scribbled a footnote about making **"a clear decision, no more**

struggle inside". Significantly, she dates the writing of the much happier *'Dreaming My Dreams'* as Christmas Day, '93, and dedicates it to her husband.

"I think these songs have a strong confrontational feel to them," she explained. *"A lot went down with the band since the first album, and a lot went down for me personally, and I think that's reflected in these songs. I couldn't really enjoy the success of the first album, because while it was happening I was having quite a bad time personally. I was really unhappy for a long time, but eventually I sorted things out. These songs came out of a period of my life that I'd like to forget, but I don't mind singing about it."*

8
everything i said

Summer 1995, and the story is even more cheering. Now it feels like The Cranberries have been around forever. Their videos always grace the TV shows. Radio DJs do amusing 'impersonations' of Dolores' voice. The band recently played an REM show. They emerge as the youngest band to play Woodstock 2 and to record an MTV *'Unplugged'* session. Oh, and they sell out London's Royal Albert Hall in the normally slack month of January, causing thousands of devotees to murmur *'Amen'* to the singer's prayer for peace in Ireland and to tearfully rhyme **"linger"** with **"finger"**.

'Ode To My Family' and *'I Can't Be With You'* have been proper hits. Every statistic about the band is monumental now. *'No Need To Argue'* has sold well over five million copies. Altogether, The Cranberries will have shifted in excess of 10 million records by the end of the year. The Daily Mirror rates Dolores as a bigger money-spinner (an estimated £3.5 million incoming in '94) than most of the women in the UK - well above the Body Shop's Anita Roderick and just behind Jackie Collins.

Meantime, Noel, Mike and Feargal literally stay out of the spotlight, passing unrecognised in the streets, seemingly unbothered that Dolores has all the glory, that her musical and songwriting input is much greater now. And while she plans on building a dream home for herself, Don and her stepson in the Gaeltacht area of County Kerry, the lads are still content to crash at their parents' places in Limerick.

For Dolores, who once wrote a famous song about the unreliability of dreams, this is a fantastic outcome. The hard-to-please music press even refers to her now as **"the last angelic innocent in an encroaching world of nastiness"**. And like all the best pop icons, she's still impossible to figure out, still a mass of contradictions.

She's the humanitarian who wants to bring back hanging. The artist who attacks the **"pea-brained Irish mentality"** but who performs a dazzling ceilidh dance for an encore. The advocate of forgiveness and love who still bangs on about rotten ex-boyfriends. A durable, strong-willed soul who likes her man to open doors for her. A sentimental girl who makes ruthless business decisions. The conservative who gets married in a shocker of a dress...

And an unarguably great singer too. What's in her head? An awful lot of things, for sure.

WOODSTOCK 94

SAUGERTIE[S]
New Yor[k]
August 13th & 14th

2 MORE DAYS of PEACE & MUSIC

FEATURING

AEROSMITH
ALLMAN BROTHERS BAND
ARRESTED DEVELOPMENT
THE BAND'S
"BIG PINK REVIEW"
(FEATURING BOB WEIR,
ROB WASSERMAN, BRUCE HORNSBY,
ROGER MCGUINN, AND HOT TUNA)
BLIND MELON
BLUES TRAVELER
CANDLEBOX
JOHNNY CASH
JIMMY CLIFF'S REGGAE JAM
(FEATURING RITA MARLEY,
DIANA KING, WORL-A-GIRL,
TOOTS AND EEK-A-MOUSE)
JOE COCKER
COLLECTIVE SOUL
SHERYL CROW
THE CRANBERRIES
CROSBY STILLS AND NASH
CYPRESS HILL
DEEE-LITE
DEL AMITRI
BOB DYLAN
MAGGIE ESTEP
MELISSA ETHERIDGE
PETER GABRIEL
REG. E. GAINES
GREEN DAY
JACKYL

JAMES
KING'S X
LIVE
METALLICA
THE NEVILLE BROTHERS
NINE INCH NAILS
THE ORB
ORBITAL
ORLEANS
PORNO FOR PYROS
PRIMUS
RED HOT CHILI PEPPERS
ROLLINS BAND
TODD RUNDGREN
SALT-N-PEPA
SANTANA
THE SISTERS OF GLORY
(FEATURING THELMA HOUSTON,
CECE PENISTON, PHOEBE SNOW,
MAVIS STAPLES AND LOIS WALDEN)
SPIN DOCTORS
TRAFFIC
VINX
VIOLENT FEMMES
W.O.M.A.D. AT WOODSTOCK
(FEATURING XALEM, THE JUSTIN TRIO,
GEOFFREY ORYEMA, HASSAN HAKMOUN)
YOUSSOU N'DOUR
ZUCCHERO
AND MORE!
ARTISTS SUBJECT TO CHANGE